Wallace Milroy's

MALT WHISKY ALMANAC

A TASTER'S GUIDE

LOCHAR PUBLISHING   MOFFAT · SCOTLAND

British Library Cataloguing in Publication Data

Milroy, Wallace
  Wallace Milroy's malt whisky almanac: a taster's guide
  1. Whiskey
  I. Title
  641.2′52   TP605

ISBN 0-948403-03-9

©Lochar Publishing 1987
Bankhead
Annan Water
MOFFAT DG10 9LS
Tel: 0683-20916

First published in July 1986
Second edition published in June 1987
Reprinted in August 1987
Edited by Neil Wilson
Designed by Grub Street Design, London
Drawings by J Lincoln Rowe
Map by Grub Street Design, London
Printed by Nevisprint Ltd, Fort William

Lochar Publishing gratefully
acknowledges the financial
assistance of United Distillers
Group and The Malt Cellar in the
production of this book.

The Malt Cellar is a collection of
six of the finest malt whiskies —
Lagavulin, Linkwood, Talisker,
Rosebank, Royal Lochnagar and
Strathconon, produced by the
United Distillers Group and
marketed in the UK by Arthur
Bell Distillers. Look for them
wherever you see The Malt Cellar cask.

CONTENTS

ACKNOWLEDGEMENTS

The author and publisher are grateful to the following
for their help in the preparation of this book: Derek
Hayward of the Ascot Cellars; Allan Stewart and Colin
Liddell of Guinness plc; Roy Macmillan and Gordon
McIntosh of the United Distillers Group; Ross Gunn,
Douglas Shaw and Mark Lawson of Seagram Distillers;
David Urquhart of Gordon & MacPhail Ltd; Mr AH
Barclay of Hiram Walker & Sons (Scotland) plc; Moyra
Peffer and Norman Wright of Whyte & Mackay
Distillers Ltd; Bill Thompson of Wm Cadenhead Ltd;
Hedley Wright of J&A Mitchell & Co Ltd; Iain Wilson
and Ann Livingston of Long John International Ltd; Mr
IM Phillips of William Lawson Distillers Ltd; Ron
Brown of The Scotch Whisky Association; Mr A
Macfarlane and Neil Gibson of William Teacher & Sons
Ltd; Simon Richmond of Arthur Bell & Sons plc; Allan
Meikle of Highland Distilleries Company plc; Peter JM
Fairlie of Glenturret Distillery Ltd; John Milroy of J
Milroy Ltd; Michael Bachelor of The Whisky Shop,
Edinburgh; Julia Thorold of Justerini & Brooks Ltd;
Ray Laughton; Decanter Magazine; Mr ECT Edwards
and Peter Enright; Alan Hall of The Wine & Spirits
Trade Club, London; Richard O'Callaghan of Takara
Shuzo & Okura & Co Ltd; Mike Don of Wm Grant &
Sons Ltd; Ken Macrae of JR Philips Ltd; Hugh Mitcalfe
and Allan Shiach of Macallan Distillers Ltd; Tim Hailey
of the Invergordon Distillers Ltd; John Grant and Tom
C Blair of J&G Grant; Pam Brough; Jim Turle of Lang
Bros; Douglas Callander of White Heather Distillers
Ltd; Sue Brown of Macdonald & Muir Ltd; George
Hocknull of Stanley P Morrison Ltd; Mrs I Scott of A
Bulloch Co Ltd and Bob Buglass of Davaar
International Ltd.

USEFUL ADDRESSES

The Scotch Whisky
Association
17 Half Moon Street
LONDON W1
Tel: 01-629-4384
Permanent displays on the
workings of a distillery
with models and Audio-
Visual. Admission free.

The Scotch Malt Whisky
Society
87 Giles Street
LEITH EH6 6BZ
Tel: 031-554-3452
Offering 10 to 20 cask
strength malts, usually
around 60% and up to 21
years old. Introductory
membership fee is £25
including a bottle of malt.

FOREWORD

To be able to drink the world's finest wines any time I felt like it, I would need an expert's knowledge constantly brought up to date, the willingness to spend unlimited time and trouble — and a considerable fortune. To pursue the finest beers at all seriously I should need to go toddling off in my private jet to breweries in England, Scotland, Germany and Scandinavia. But to have the world's finest spirit in my glass at a minute's notice I need no more than an ordinary drinker's income and a modest stock of information.

Twenty years ago, to the vast majority of mankind, 'the finest spirit in the world' could only have meant brandy, and brandy from the district of Cognac at that, above all but the lowest grades, steeply or very steeply priced. Now, the amazing growth in the standing and popularity of Scotch malt whisky has changed that picture for ever. For myself I can only say that the best malts seem at least the equals of any brandy I have ever been able to afford, that they altogether lack the uncomfortable side-effects brandy can have, and that their range of style, flavour, aroma and everything else is much wider.

So wide, in fact, that even those of us who have enjoyably learnt something of the subject for ourselves need education and guidance. That great authority, Professor R.J.S. McDowall, has written that Scotch whiskies are 'as varied as the wines of France'. I first read those words in 1975, and every year I have found further evidence of their truth.

This is where Wallace Milroy comes in. He has a proper enthusiasm, a professional's command of this vast and pleasurable field of knowledge, and a marvellous ability to distil the fruits of his experience into a few practical words.

Kingsley Amis

INTRODUCTION

This Almanac was first published because malt whiskies were no longer the domain of an exclusive body of academic tasters and connoisseurs, but were to be found in increasing numbers in supermarkets, wine shops and duty free outlets at home and abroad. As distillers continue to budget greater amounts on the marketing of their malts, the public are at last getting access to a national asset as valuable to Scotland as the brandy houses are to France.

The market continues to look promising for malt sales worldwide, but, due to the over-production of the 1970s, a great many malt distilleries are still closed or "mothballed", a situation which the brandy houses of France are not experiencing. With such a buoyant market this may not appear so serious, but continuing closure causes deeper and irreversible effects. For instance, it is malt from a variety of distilleries that, when blended with grain whisky, imparts the flavour which distinguishes each popular brand. Thus the blender's most valuable ingredient is slowly whittled away, ultimately reducing the pleasure which Scotch drinkers the world over have received for over a hundred years. It is not by whim that generations of master blenders have carefully selected precise proportions of malt — be sure that they regard them as indispensable.

Many of Scotland's malts are produced in small, remote communities where the loss of income due to closure is felt not only by the workforce, but also the local shops and services. Only by capturing greater market shares can the producers hope to stave off that most unpleasant scenario — the day when a distillery and its malt becomes a memory.

This revised edition is presented in a slightly new format to take into account company restructuring, new malts (I welcome The Singleton of Auchroisk), old ones that are no longer available (sadly, Banff is now a memory) and my desire to see you adding your own comments on the malts you are trying. Each malt is now entered on its own page, where space is available for you to make your own notes — except in a few cases where the already considerable amount of information means that you have to add your notes on pages 118 and 119.

The Almanac contains 106 malts of which 64 are brands and the remainder are available from the two main independent bottlers at a variety of ages and strength. The age is usually marked on the label but may not be shown as some producers prefer to bottle their malts as and when they are considered ready. Strength is always given and is normally shown as a percentage of alcohol by volume, most commonly 40%. This is equivalent to 80° proof in the United States.

The language of the taster is not really susceptible to change, since the product is basically the same with variations on the theme. My own view is that the wine taster's terms — marvellously descriptive of his own subject — simply don't apply to Scotch, or if they are applied too lightly, are misleading. What might be instructive to us all, amateur and professional alike, would be a taster's back-label on each bottle to see what the distillers honestly think of their own products. I probably wouldn't agree with all their opinions, and you may not with mine, so record your own as you work your way through the malts in this Almanac. It will make your enviable task all the easier as you discover what I did many years ago . . . that there is nothing quite like it.

THE MALT WHISKY PRODUCING REGIONS OF SCOTLAND

ORKNEY

Outer Hebrides

Wick●

SKYE

NORTHERN

●Elgin

●Inverness

SPEYSIDE

HIGHLAND

Aberdeen●

●Fort William

EASTERN

ISLAND

MULL

WESTERN

SOUTHERN

●Dundee

Oban●

JURA

ISLAY

●Glasgow

●Edinburgh

CAMPBELTOWN LOWLAND

●Dumfries

Barton International Ltd

52 - 58 Weston St, LONDON SE1 3QJ

Tel: 01-407-2922

Brand	# GLEN SCOTIA
Distillery	Glen Scotia CAMPBELTOWN, Argyll
Licensees	A Gillies & Co (Distillers) Ltd
Reception centre	No
Producing region	Campbeltown
Age when bottled	8 years
Strength	40%

TASTING NOTES

Nose	Faint touch of smoke. Intense aroma, but still delicate and sweet
Taste	Light for a Campbeltown. Hint of peat with a good finish.
Comments	Pre-dinner dram. In fact, a good drink at any time.

PERSONAL NOTES

Brand	LITTLEMILL
Distillery	Littlemill BOWLING, Dunbartonshire
Licensees	Barton International Ltd
Reception centre	No
Producing region	Lowland
Age when bottled	5 & 8 years
Strength	40%

TASTING NOTES *(8 year old)*

Nose	Light and delicate.
Taste	Mellow-flavoured, light, slightly cloying yet pleasant and warming..
Comments	Pre-dinner, from a distillery full of interesting, novel features.

PERSONAL NOTES

Glen Catrine Bonded Warehouse Ltd

Laigh Rd, CATRINE, Ayrshire KA5 6SQ

Tel: 0290-51211

Brand	**INCHMURRIN**
Distillery	Loch Lomond ALEXANDRIA, Dunbartonshire
Licensees	Glen Catrine Bonded Warehouse Ltd
Reception centre	No
Producing region	Highland, Southern
Age when bottled	None given
Strength	40%

TASTING NOTES

Nose	Slightly aromatic. Follows through on the palate.
Taste	Light-bodied. Most of the flavour is on the front of the palate and thus finishes quickly.
Comments	A good everyday drinking malt. Pre-dinner. Until recently owned by ADP and then Inverhouse Distillers, the distillery now produces two malts from stills similar to those at Littlemill. **Old Rhosdhu** will shortly be introduced to the home market. *(PERSONAL NOTES — page 119).*

Glenturret Distillery Ltd

CRIEFF, Perthshire PH7 4HA

Tel: 0764-2424

Brand	THE GLENTURRET
Distillery	Glenturret The Hosh, CRIEFF, Perthshire PH7 4HA
Licensees	Glenturret Distillery Ltd
Reception Centre	Yes. Very popular. Award Winning Heritage Centre with audio-visual. Exhibition Museum, tasting bar and restaurant.
Producing region	Highland, Southern
Age when bottled	8, 12, 15 & 21 years
Strength	40%

TASTING NOTES *(12 year old)*

Nose	Very impressive aromatic nose.
Taste	Full, lush body with a good depth of flavour and a stimulating finish. Delightful.
Comments	An award winning malt from Scotland's oldest distillery, where the cat 'Towser' which died aged 23 in March 1987, held the world mouse-catching record — over 27,890! *(PERSONAL NOTES — page 119).*

J&G Grant

Glenfarclas Distillery, Marypark

BALLINDALLOCH, Banffshire AB3 9BD

Tel: 08072-245

Brand	GLENFARCLAS
Distillery	Glenfarclas Marypark, BALLINDALLOCH Banffshire
Licensees	J&G Grant
Reception centre	Yes, a very informative one with free tastings.
Producing region	Highland, Speyside
Age when bottled	8, 10, 12, 15, 21 & 25 years
Strength	8 year old — 60% ('105') 10 year old — 40% 15 year old — 46% 12, 21 & 25 year old — 43%

TASTING NOTES	*(15 year old, 46%)*
Nose	A rich, delicious promise (which is fulfilled).
Taste	Full of character and flavour, one of the great Highland malts.
Comments	A superb after-dinner dram. *(PERSONAL NOTES — page 118).*

Wm Grant & Sons Ltd

206 - 208 West George St, GLASGOW G2 2PE

Tel: 041-248-3101

Brand	THE BALVENIE
Distillery	Balvenie
	DUFFTOWN, Banffshire
Licensees	Wm Grant & Sons Ltd
Reception centre	No
Producing region	Highland, Speyside
Age when bottled	8 years minimum
Strength	40%

TASTING NOTES

Nose	Excellent well-pronounced aroma.
Taste	Big, distinctive flavour with a sweet aftertaste.
Comments	A connoisseur's malt for after-dinner.

PERSONAL NOTES

Brand	**GLENFIDDICH**
Distillery	Glenfiddich DUFFTOWN, Banffshire
Licensees	Wm Grant & Sons Ltd
Reception centre	Yes, very popular.
Producing region	Highland, Speyside
Age when bottled	8 years minimum
Strength	40%

TASTING NOTES

Nose	A light, delicate touch of peat.
Taste	Attractive flavour, with an after-sweetness. Well balanced. A good introductory malt.
Comments	If you have never tasted a malt, start with this one.

PERSONAL NOTES

The Highland Distilleries Co PLC

106 West Nile St, GLASGOW G1 2QY

Tel: 041-332-7511

Brand	**BUNNAHABHAIN** *(Bu-na-ha-van)*
Distillery	Bunnahabhain PORT ASKAIG, Islay, Argyll
Licensees	The Highland Distilleries Co PLC
Reception centre	No, but visitors are always welcome. Tel: 049684-646.
Producing region	Islay *(Eye-la)*
Age when bottled	12 years
Strength	40%

TASTING NOTES

Nose	Pronounced character with a flowery aroma.
Taste	Not reminiscent of the Islay style, but a lovely round flavour nonetheless.
Comments	A popular after-dinner dram gaining new friends in France and the United States.

PERSONAL NOTES

Malt	GLENGLASSAUGH
Distillery	Glenglassaugh PORTSOY, Banffshire
Licensees	The Highland Distilleries Co PLC
Reception centre	No
Producing region	Highland, Speyside

TASTING NOTES *(1967 distillation)*

Nose	Pleasant and fresh.
Taste	Medium to full-bodied on the palate tending to be slightly dry with a good follow-through.
Comments	Available only from the independent bottlers (see page 116).

PERSONAL NOTES

Malt	GLENROTHES
Distillery	Glenrothes ROTHES, Morayshire
Licensees	Glenrothes-Glenlivet Ltd
Reception centre	No
Producing region	Highland, Speyside

TASTING NOTES *(8 year old, 40%)*

Nose	Fruity, pleasant.
Taste	Medium, well rounded flavour with a hint of dryness. Balance lends a smooth effect.
Comments	Again, only available from the independent bottlers (see page 117).

PERSONAL NOTES

Single Malt Scotch Whisky

DISTILLED AND BOTTLED BY JAMES GRANT AND CO.
(HIGHLAND PARK DISTILLERY) LTD. KIRKWALL ORKNEY SCOTLAND

PRODUCT OF SCOTLAND

Brand	HIGHLAND PARK
Distillery	Highland Park KIRKWALL, Orkney
Licensees	James Grant & Co (Highland Park Distillery) Ltd
Reception centre	Yes. Tel: 0856-4619.
Producing region	Island, Orkney
Age when bottled	12 years
Strength	40%

TASTING NOTES

Nose	Full of character — pleasant, lingering and smokey.
Taste	Medium, well balanced flavour finishing with a subtle dryness.
Comments	An excellent after-dinner dram from Scotland's most northerly distillery.

PERSONAL NOTES

Brand	TAMDHU *(Tamm-doo)*
Distillery	Tamdhu KNOCKANDO, Morayshire
Licensees	Tamdhu-Glenlivet Ltd
Reception centre	Yes. Tel: 03406-221.
Producing region	Highland, Speyside
Age when bottled	10 years
Strength	40%

TASTING NOTES

Nose	Light aroma with a trace of sweetness.
Taste	Medium, with a little sweetness and a very mellow finish.
Comments	A good after-dinner dram which is both popular and readily available.

PERSONAL NOTES

International Distillers & Vintners Ltd

1 York Gate, LONDON NW1 4PU

Tel: 01-487-3412

Brand	GLEN SPEY
Distillery	Glen Spey ROTHES, Morayshire
Licensees	Gilbey Vintners Ltd
Reception centre	No
Producing region	Highland, Speyside
Age when bottled	8 years
Strength	40%

TASTING NOTES

Nose	Light, fragrant and delicate.
Taste	Very smooth and fragrant. A good all-round drink.
Comments	Pre-dinner.

PERSONAL NOTES

Brand	**THE SINGLETON OF AUCHROISK**
Distillery	Auchroisk MULBEN, Banffshire
Licensees	Ruchill & Ross Ltd
Reception centre	No
Producing region	Highland, Speyside
Age when bottled	12 years
Strength	40%

TASTING NOTES

Nose	Distinctive, attractive bouquet with a touch of fruit.
Taste	Medium-weight, hint of sweetness with a delicious long-lasting flavour.
Comments	After-dinner. A new malt from a "new" distillery opened in 1974 and very welcome too. A charmer.

PERSONAL NOTES

The Invergordon Distillers Ltd

9-21 Salamander Place, Leith

EDINBURGH EH6 7JL

Tel: 031-554-4404

Brand	**BRUICHLADDICH** *(Broo-ick-laddie)*
Distillery	Bruichladdich BRUICHLADDICH, Islay, Argyll
Licensees	Bruichladdich Distillery Co Ltd
Reception centre	No, but visitors are always welcome. Tel: 049685-221.
Producing region	Islay
Age when bottled	10 years
Strength	40%

TASTING NOTES

Nose	Light to medium with a hint of peat.
Taste	Lingering flavour giving the expected fullness of Islay character whilst lacking the heavier tones.
Comments	A good pre-dinner dram. *(PERSONAL NOTES — page 118).*

Brand	**DEANSTON**
Distillery	Deanston DOUNE, Perthshire
Licensees	Deanston Distilleries Ltd
Reception centre	No
Producing region	Highland, Perthshire
Age when bottled	None given
Strength	40%

TASTING NOTES

Nose	A hint of sweetness.
Taste	Light, finishes with a smooth trace of sweetness.
Comments	A pre-dinner malt, from a distillery which used to be a cotton mill until 1965.

PERSONAL NOTES

Brand	GLENALLACHIE
Distillery	Glenallachie ABERLOUR, Banffshire
Licensees	Glenallachie Distillery Co Ltd
Reception centre	No
Producing region	Highland, Speyside
Age when bottled	12 years
Strength	40%, 43% for export

TASTING NOTES

Nose	Very elegant with a delightful bouquet.
Taste	Smooth bodied with a lovely, light sweet finish. Extremely well balanced.
Comments	A recent acquisition from Charles Mackinlay & Co Ltd . . . and what a good one.

PERSONAL NOTES

Brand	**ISLE OF JURA**
Distillery	Isle of Jura Craighouse, JURA, Argyll
Licensees	Isle of Jura Distillery Co Ltd
Reception centre	No, but visitors are welcome. Tel: 049682-240.
Producing region	Island, Jura
Age when bottled	8 & 10 years
Strength	40%

TASTING NOTES (8 year old)

Nose	Smooth with subtle peaty traces. Dry.
Taste	Well matured, full but delicate flavour. Good lingering character.
Comments	An almost Highland-like malt for drinking anytime. Acquired at the same time as Glenallachie. Always worth visiting the distillery.

PERSONAL NOTES

Brand	TAMNAVULIN
	(Tamna-voolin)
Distillery	Tamnavulin
	BALLINDALLOCH, Banffshire
Licensees	The Tamnavulin-Glenlivet
	Distillery Co Ltd
Reception centre	Yes. A charming old mill with a
	beautiful sheltered picnic area.
Producing region	Highland, Speyside
Age when bottled	10 years
Strength	40%

TASTING NOTES

Nose	Well matured, mellow, with a hint of sweetness.
Taste	Medium weight with a light, smokey, pronounced finish.
Comments	A good all-round malt.

PERSONAL NOTES

Brand	**TULLIBARDINE** *(Tully-bardeen)*
Distillery	Tullibardine BLACKFORD, Perthshire
Licensees	Tullibardine Distillery Co Ltd
Reception centre	No
Producing region	Highland, Southern
Age when bottled	10 years
Strength	40%

TASTING NOTES

Nose	Delicate, mellow, sweet aroma.
Taste	Full-bodied, with a fruity flavour and good lingering taste.
Comments	A pre-dinner dram.

PERSONAL NOTES

Justerini & Brooks Ltd

17 Cornwall Terrace, LONDON NW1 4QP

Tel: 01-486-7272

Brand	KNOCKANDO
Distillery	Knockando KNOCKANDO, Morayshire
Licensees	Justerini and Brooks Ltd
Reception Centre	No
Producing region	Highland, Speyside
Age when bottled	10-15 years
Strength	40%

TASTING NOTES

Nose	Full and pleasant.
Taste	Medium-bodied, with a finish reminiscent of sugar almonds.
Comments	After-dinner. Bottled when it is considered ready, rather than at a pre-determined age. The label carries dates of distillation and bottling.

PERSONAL NOTES

Lang Brothers Ltd

100 West Nile St, GLASGOW G1 2QT

Tel: 041-332-6361

Brand	GLENGOYNE
Distillery	Glengoyne DUMGOYNE, Stirlingshire
Licensees	Lang Brothers Ltd
Reception centre	Yes. Tel: 041-332-6361.
Producing region	Highland, Southern
Age when bottled	10, 12 & 17 years
Strength	10 year old — 40% 12 year old (Export & Duty Free) — 43% 17 year old — 43%

TASTING NOTES (10 year old)

Nose	A light, fresh aroma.
Taste	Light, pleasant all-round malt.
Comments	Another great introduction to malts. The newly-introduced 17 year old will gain many friends.

PERSONAL NOTES

William Lawson Distillers Ltd

288 Main Street, COATBRIDGE ML5 3RH

Tel: 0236-22651

Brand	GLEN DEVERON
Distillery	Macduff BANFF, Banffshire
Licensees	Wm Lawson Distillers Ltd
Reception centre	No
Producing region	Highland, Speyside
Age when bottled	12 years
Strength	40%

TASTING NOTES

Nose	A pronounced, refreshing bouquet.
Taste	Medium weight with a smooth pleasant flavour and a clean finish.
Comments	After-dinner dram, also available from the independent bottlers as **Macduff,** distilled in 1963 (see page 117, and make ***PERSONAL NOTES*** on page 118).

Long John International Ltd

123 - 157 Bothwell St, GLASGOW G2 7AY

Tel: 041-248-4201

Malt	BEN NEVIS
Distillery	Ben Nevis FORT WILLIAM, Inverness-shire
Licensees	Ben Nevis (Fort William) Distillery Ltd
Reception centre	No
Producing region	Highland, Western

TASTING NOTES (19 year old, 46%)

Nose	Curious, ripe fruit nose.
Taste	Round flavour of no great character but good for beginners.
Comments	Tasting sample not typical of the current product. From the independent bottlers (see page 116).

PERSONAL NOTES

Bowmore Distillery (see page 43)

Malt	GLENUGIE
Distillery	Glenugie PETERHEAD, Aberdeenshire (no longer licensed)
Producing region	Highland, Eastern

TASTING NOTES (20 year old, 46%)

Nose	Hint of ripe fruit.
Taste	Initial trace of sweetness, firm, malty but with a quick, dry finish.
Comments	Pre-dinner from the independent bottlers (see page 117).

PERSONAL NOTES

Malt	**KINCLAITH**
Distillery	Kinclaith (dismantled 1975)
Producing region	Lowland

TASTING NOTES *(18 year old, 46%)*

Nose	Light and smokey with a spirit sharpness.
Taste	Full-bodied, smooth with an attractive finish.
Comments	From the independent bottlers (see page 117).

PERSONAL NOTES

LAPHROAIG®

UNBLENDED
ISLAY MALT SCOTCH WHISKY

10 years old

The most richly flavoured of
all Scotch whiskies

DISTILLED AND BOTTLED IN SCOTLAND BY
D. JOHNSTON & CO. (LAPHROAIG) LTD, LAPHROAIG DISTILLERY, ISLE OF ISLAY.

40%vol   75cl

Brand	LAPHROAIG *(La-froyg)*
Distillery	Laphroaig PORT ELLEN, Islay, Argyll
Licensees	D Johnston & Co Ltd
Reception centre	No, but visitors are always welcome. Tel: 0496-2418.
Producing region	Islay
Age when bottled	10 & 15 years
Strength	40%, up to 45.1% for export.

TASTING NOTES *(10 year old)*

Nose	Well balanced, peaty-smokey.
Taste	Full of character. Big Islay peaty flavour with a delightful touch of sweetness. Betrays its proximity to the sea.
Comments	An excellent after dinner malt from a beautifully situated distillery. Very popular.

PERSONAL NOTES

Brand	TORMORE
Distillery	Tormore Advie, GRANTOWN-ON-SPEY, Morayshire
Licensees	Long John International Ltd
Reception centre	No, but visitors are welcome.
Producing region	Highland, Speyside
Age when bottled	10 years, and 5 years for export.
Strength	40%, up to 43% for export.

TASTING NOTES

Nose	Nicely defined dry aroma.
Taste	Medium-bodied with a hint of sweetness and a pleasant, lingering aftertaste.
Comments	After-dinner.

PERSONAL NOTES

The Macallan Distillers Ltd

CRAIGELLACHIE, Banffshire AB3 9RX

Tel: 03405-471

Brand	THE MACALLAN
Distillery	Macallan CRAIGELLACHIE, Banffshire
Licensees	The Macallan Distillers Ltd
Reception centre	Yes. By appointment only.
Producing region	Highland, Speyside
Age when bottled	UK market — 10, 18 (currently 1968 distillation) & 25 years old. Export market — 10, 12, 18 & 25 years old. Italian market — 7 years old.
Strength	7 & 10 year old — 40%, with some 10 year old at 57%; 25 year old, 1968 distillation and export bottlings — 43%.

TASTING NOTES (10 year old)

Nose	Smooth aroma with a silky bouquet.
Taste	Full, delightful and sherried with a beautiful lingering aftertaste.
Comments	A masterpiece. All Macallan is casked in sherrywood. *(PERSONAL NOTES — page 119).*

Macdonald & Muir Ltd

Macdonald House, 186 Commercial St, Leith

EDINBURGH EH6 6NN

Tel: 031-554-4477

Brand	**GLENMORANGIE**
Distillery	Glenmorangie TAIN, Ross-shire
Licensees	The Glenmorangie Distillery Co
Reception centre	No
Producing region	Highland, Northern
Age when bottled	10 years
Strength	40%

TASTING NOTES

Nose	Beautiful aroma. Fresh and sweet with a subtle hint of peat.
Taste	Medium-bodied with a sweet, fresh finish. One to linger and dwell upon.
Comments	An excellent malt, very popular. Remember to prounounce the name as **orangey.** The best-selling malt in Scotland. *(PERSONAL NOTES — page 118).*

Brand	**GLEN MORAY**
Distillery	Glen Moray ELGIN, Morayshire
Licensees	The Glen Moray-Glenlivet Distillery Co Ltd
Reception centre	No
Producing region	Highland, Speyside
Age when bottled	12 years
Strength	40%

TASTING NOTES

Nose	Fresh, light aroma.
Taste	Light, pleasant and malty with a clean finish. A fine all-round malt.
Comments	A pre-dinner dram, beautifully presented.

PERSONAL NOTES

J&A Mitchell & Co Ltd

Springbank Distillery, CAMPBELTOWN

Argyll PA28 6ET

Tel: 05865-2085

Brand	**LONGROW**
Distillery	Springbank CAMPBELTOWN, Argyll
Licensees	J&A Mitchell & Co Ltd
Reception centre	No
Producing region	Campbeltown
Age when bottled	12 years old (export also).
Strength	46%

TASTING NOTES

Nose	Peaty, smokey.
Taste	Well balanced, with a hint of sweetness. A creamy, malty palate and a fine lingering aftertaste. Almost an Islay.
Comments	Distilled at Springbank, but by using entirely peat-dried malted barley, the heavier peated malt results. *(PERSONAL NOTES — page 119).*

Brand	SPRINGBANK
Distillery	Springbank CAMPBELTOWN, Argyll
Licensees	J&A Mitchell & Co Ltd
Reception centre	No
Producing region	Campbeltown
Age when bottled	12, 15, 21 & 30 years. Export: 8, 10, 12, 15, 21 & 33 years.
Strength	12, 15, 21 & 30 years old — 46%; 12 year old — 57%. Export: 8, 10, 12, 15 & 21 years old — 43%; 33 year old — 46%.

TASTING NOTES *(21 year old, 46%)*

Nose	Steadfast, with a pronounced aroma and a slight sweetness.
Taste	Well balanced, full of charm and elegance. A malt drinker's dream.
Comments	Largest selling malt in Japan. Superb after-dinner drink — you won't refuse the second one! Bottled at the distillery and now widely available. *(PERSONAL NOTES — page 119).*

Stanley P Morrison Ltd

Springburn Bond, Carlisle St

GLASGOW G21 1EQ

Tel: 041-558-9011

Brand	AUCHENTOSHAN
Distillery	Auchentoshan DUNTOCHER, Dunbartonshire
Licensees	Stanley P Morrison Ltd
Reception centre	Yes, currently handling 40,000 visitors per annum and to be expanded.
Producing region	Lowland
Age when bottled	10, 12 & 18 years.
Strength	40%, 43% for export.

TASTING NOTES (10 year old)

Nose	Delicate, slightly sweet.
Taste	Light, soft sweetness with a good aftertaste.
Comments	A triple-distilled malt from one of Scotland's most visited distilleries. Popular and readily available at home and abroad. *(PERSONAL NOTES — page 118).*

Brand	**BOWMORE**
Distillery	Bowmore BOWMORE, Islay, Argyll
Licensees	Bowmore Distillery Co Ltd
Reception centre	Yes, the best in the islands. Tel: 049681-441.
Producing region	Islay
Age when bottled	12 years
Strength	40%, 43% for export.

TASTING NOTES

Nose	Light, peaty-smokey.
Taste	Healthy, middle-range Islay with medium weight and a smooth finish.
Comments	Popular after-dinner malt selling very well in all the UK duty free outlets. Some of the older sherry-casked bottlings are outstanding. Distillery is well worth visiting.

PERSONAL NOTES

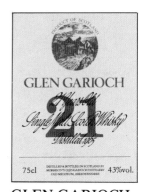

Brand	**GLEN GARIOCH** *(Glen-geerie)*
Distillery	Glen Garioch OLDMELDRUM, Aberdeenshire
Licensees	The Glen Garioch Whisky Co Ltd
Reception centre	Yes. Tel: 06512-2706.
Producing region	Highland, Eastern
Age when bottled	10 & 21 years
Strength	10 year old — 40% 21 year old — 43%

TASTING NOTES (21 year old)

Nose	Delicate and smokey.
Taste	Pronounced peaty flavour with a smooth, pleasant finish.
Comments	Good introductory malt, beautifully presented with an award-winning advertising campaign behind it. Distillery utilises waste heat to cultivate tomatoes and pot-plants!

PERSONAL NOTES

Ricard International SA

S.E.G.M., Rue de Solserino, 75007 PARIS

FRANCE

Brand	ABERLOUR
Distillery	Aberlour ABERLOUR, Banffshire
Licensees	Aberlour-Glenlivet Distillery Co Ltd
Reception centre	No
Producing region	Highland, Speyside
Age when bottled	12 years
Strength	40%

TASTING NOTES

Nose	Rich, delightful aroma.
Taste	A fine, smooth, lingering texture.
Comments	Good after-dinner dram, becoming popular in France and Italy.

PERSONAL NOTES

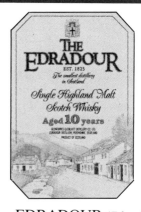

Brand	EDRADOUR *(Edra-dower)*
Distillery	Edradour PITLOCHRY, Perthshire
Licensees	William Whiteley & Co Ltd
Reception centre	Yes. Tel: 0796-2095.
Producing region	Highland, Southern
Age when bottled	10 years
Strength	40%

TASTING NOTES *(18 year old, 46%)*

Nose	Fruity-sweet and smokey.
Taste	Creamy, smooth and malty with a tinge of dryness and a good aftertaste.
Comments	Scotland's smallest distillery and therefore closest to a working 19th-century distillery. Well worth a visit.

PERSONAL NOTES

The Seagram Company Ltd

1430 Peel Street, MONTREAL, Quebec,

CANADA

Malt	BENRIACH
Distillery	Benriach Longmorn, ELGIN, Morayshire
Licensees	The Seagram Co Ltd
Reception centre	No
Producing region	Highland, Speyside

TASTING NOTES (13 year old, 46%)

Nose	Light, elusive, delicate.
Taste	Medium flavour and taste that takes time to come through on the palate.
Comments	A pre-dinner dram from the independent bottlers (see page 116).

PERSONAL NOTES

Malt	CAPERDONICH
Distillery	Caperdonich ROTHES, Morayshire
Licensees	The Seagram Co Ltd
Reception centre	No
Producing region	Highland, Speyside

TASTING NOTES *(14 year old, 46%)*

Nose	A light, very delicate fragrance of peat.
Taste	Medium, slight hint of fruit with a quick smokey finish.
Comments	Only from the independent bottlers (see page 116). The distillery is across the road from Glen Grant and used to be called Glen Grant No 2.

PERSONAL NOTES

Brand	GLEN GRANT
Distillery	Glen Grant ROTHES, Morayshire
Licensees	The Seagram Co Ltd
Reception centre	Yes. Tel: 03403-413.
Producing region	Highland, Speyside
Age when bottled	UK market — none given. Export market — 5 years old (Italy), 10 years old and none given.
Strength	40%

TASTING NOTES

Nose	Light, dry aroma.
Taste	Dry flavour, light — another good all-round malt.
Comments	Pre-dinner.

PERSONAL NOTES

Malt	**GLEN KEITH**
Distillery	Glen Keith KEITH, Banffshire
Licensees	The Seagram Co Ltd
Reception centre	No
Producing region	Highland, Speyside

TASTING NOTES *(17 year old, 46%)*

Nose	Light, sweet and attractive.
Taste	Light, with a hint of fruit. Smooth and well rounded.
Comments	Pre-dinner, from the independent bottlers (see page 116).

PERSONAL NOTES

Brand	**LONGMORN**
Distillery	Longmorn Longmorn, ELGIN, Morayshire
Licensees	The Seagram Co Ltd
Reception centre	No
Producing region	Highland, Speyside
Age when bottled	15 years
Strength	43%

TASTING NOTES

Nose	A delightful, fragrant bouquet.
Taste	Full-bodied, fleshy, nutty, lots of character.
Comments	Re-introduced at this age in 1986 by marketers Hill, Thomson & Co — at last the public can appreciate this classic after-dinner malt. Outstanding.

PERSONAL NOTES

Brand	STRATHISLA *(Strath-eye-la)*
Distillery	Strathisla KEITH, Banffshire
Licensees	The Seagram Co Ltd
Reception centre	Yes
Producing region	Highland, Speyside
Age when bottled	12 years
Strength	40%

TASTING NOTES

Nose	Beautiful, bewitching fragrance of fruit which also reflects the taste to come.
Taste	Slender hint of sweetness with an extremely long, lingering fullness. Good balance.
Comments	An exellent after-dinner malt — one of the best to sip and savour. Distilled and bottled by Chivas Brothers Ltd.

PERSONAL NOTES

Brand	THE GLENLIVET
Distillery	The Glenlivet MINMORE, Banffshire
Licensees	The Seagram Co Ltd
Reception centre	Yes. Tel: 08073-427.
Producing region	Highland, Speyside
Age when bottled	12 years
Strength	40%, 43% for export.

TASTING NOTES

Nose	A light, delicate nose with lots of fruit.
Taste	Medium-light trace of sweetness, quite full on the palate — a first class malt.
Comments	This one never disappoints. Popular and available everywhere.

PERSONAL NOTES

Takara Shuzo & Okura & Co Ltd

TOMATIN, Inverness-shire IV13 7YT

Tel: 08082-234

Brand	TOMATIN
Distillery	Tomatin TOMATIN, Inverness-shire
Licensees	The Tomatin Distillery Company Ltd
Reception centre	No, but visitors are welcome. Tel: 08082-234.
Producing region	Highland, Northern
Age when bottled	5 & 10 years
Strength	40%, 43% for export

TASTING NOTES (10 years, 40%)

Nose	Pleasant and light.
Taste	Light body, very smooth.
Comments	A pre-dinner dram and a good introduction to malt whisky. The distillery was the first to be acquired by the Japanese in 1985.

PERSONAL NOTES

William Teacher & Sons Ltd

St Enoch Square, GLASGOW G1 4BZ

Tel: 041-204-2633

Malt	ARDMORE
Distillery	Ardmore KENNETHMONT Aberdeenshire
Licensees	Wm Teacher & Sons Ltd
Reception centre	No
Producing region	Highland, Speyside

TASTING NOTES (18 year old, 46%)

Nose	A light aroma.
Taste	Big, sweet and malty on the palate with a good, crisp finish.
Comments	Only from the independent bottlers (see page 116). After-dinner.

PERSONAL NOTES

Brand	**GLENDRONACH**
Distillery	Glendronach Forgue, by HUNTLY Aberdeenshire
Licensees	Wm Teacher & Sons Ltd
Reception centre	Yes
Producing region	Highland, Speyside
Age when bottled	12 years (Original or Sherrywood)
Strength	40%, 43% for export.

TASTING NOTES *(Sherrywood)*

Nose	Smooth aroma with a light trace of sweetness.
Taste	Well balanced, lingering on the palate with a delicious, decisive after-taste.
Comments	A good dram, after-dinner. Will definitely be sought-after.

PERSONAL NOTES

Tobermory Distillers Ltd

St John's Place, CLECKHEATON

West Yorkshire

Tel: 0274-873351

Brand	TOBERMORY *(formerly Ledaig)*
Distillery	Tobermory TOBERMORY, Mull, Argyll
Licensees	Tobermory Distillers Ltd
Reception centre	No
Producing region	Island, Mull
Age when bottled	None given
Strength	40%

TASTING NOTES

Nose	Fine, fruity nose.
Taste	Gentle flavour with a soft finish. A good, subtle malt.
Comments	Pre-dinner, from a distillery with a fascinating history. Also available from the independent bottlers under its old name **Ledaig** (see page 117).

PERSONAL NOTES

United Distillers Group

33 Ellersly Road

EDINBURGH EH12 6JW

Tel: 031-337-7373

Editors note: Any enquiries regarding the malts produced by United Distillers Group should be directed to:
Arthur Bell Distillers
Cherrybank, PERTH PH2 0NG
Tel: 0738-21111

Being the home trade marketing company of United Distillers Group, the spirits subsidiary of Guinness PLC.

Malt	**ABERFELDY**
Distillery	Aberfeldy ABERFELDY, Perthshire
Licensees	John Dewar & Sons Ltd
Reception centre	Provisional. Tel: 0887-20330.
Producing region	Highland, Southern

TASTING NOTES *(1969 Distillation)*

Nose	Fresh, clean with a lightly peated nose.
Taste	Nice substantial flavour with a good round taste.
Comments	From the independent bottlers (see page 116).

PERSONAL NOTES

Brand	AULTMORE
Distillery	Aultmore KEITH, Banffshire
Licensees	John and Robert Harvey & Co Ltd
Reception Centre	No
Producing region	Highland, Speyside
Age when bottled	12 years
Strength	40%

TASTING NOTES

Nose	A delightful fresh aroma with a sweet hint and a touch of peat.
Taste	Smooth, well balanced with a mellow, warming finish.
Comments	Available readily and suitable as an after-dinner malt.

PERSONAL NOTES

Malt	BALMENACH
Distillery	Balmenach Cromdale, GRANTOWN-ON-SPEY, Morayshire
Licensees	John Crabbie & Co Ltd
Reception centre	No
Producing region	Highland, Speyside

TASTING NOTES (24 year old, 46%)

Nose	Light but attractive.
Taste	Slight spirit flavour with a quick, but full, finish.
Comments	A pre-dinner dram available from the independent bottlers (see page 116).

PERSONAL NOTES

Laphroaig Distillery (see page 35)

Malt	BENRINNES
Distillery	Benrinnes ABERLOUR, Banffshire
Licensees	A&A Crawford Ltd
Reception centre	No
Producing region	Highland, Speyside

TASTING NOTES (18 year old, 46%)

Nose	A pleasant delicate hint of peat.
Taste	Subtle, fine flavour which gradually catches up on the tastebuds.
Comments	Pre-dinner, but only available from the independent bottlers (see page 116).

PERSONAL NOTES

Malt	BENROMACH
Distillery	Benromach FORRES, Morayshire
Licensees	J&W Hardie Ltd
Reception centre	No
Producing region	Highland

TASTING NOTES (14 year old, 46%)

Nose	Light, delicate and attractive.
Taste	Light and delicate but finishes with a pronounced spirit taste.
Comments	Only available from the independent bottlers (see page 116). Pre-dinner.

PERSONAL NOTES

Brand	BLADNOCH
Distillery	Bladnoch BLADNOCH, Wigtownshire
Licensees	Arthur Bell & Sons PLC
Reception centre	No
Producing region	Lowland
Age when bottled	8 years
Strength	40%

TASTING NOTES

Nose	Very light and delicate.
Taste	Smooth, delicate but full and easy to drink.
Comments	Scotland's most southerly distillery. A pre-dinner malt gaining in popularity since acquisition by Bell in 1983.

PERSONAL NOTES

Brand	**BLAIR ATHOL**
Distillery	Blair Athol PITLOCHRY, Perthshire
Licensees	Arthur Bell & Sons PLC
Reception centre	Yes (trade only)
Producing region	Highland, Southern
Age when bottled	8 years
Strength	40%

TASTING NOTES

Nose	Light, fresh, clean aroma.
Taste	Medium hint of peat with a nice round finish. Plenty of flavour.
Comments	Pre-dinner, readily available.

PERSONAL NOTES

Malt	CAOL ILA *(Kaol-eela)*
Distillery	Caol Ila PORT ASKAIG, Islay, Argyll
Licensees	Bulloch, Lade & Co Ltd
Reception centre	No. Visiting by appointment. Tel: 049684-207.
Producing region	Islay

TASTING NOTES *(1969 distillation)*

Nose	Light, fresh with a trace of peat.
Taste	Not a heavy Islay, but has pleasing weight and a fairly round flavour. Finishes smoothly.
Comments	Popular pre-dinner dram, readily available from the independent bottlers (see page 116). Distillery is spectacularly situated on the Sound of Islay.

PERSONAL NOTES

Caol Ila Distillery

Brand	**CARDHU** *(Kaar-doo)*
Distillery	Cardhu KNOCKANDO, Morayshire
Licensees	John Walker & Sons Ltd
Reception centre	Yes. Tel: 03406-204.
Producing region	Highland, Speyside
Age when bottled	12 years
Strength	40%

TASTING NOTES

Nose	A hint of sweetness with an excellent bouquet.
Taste	Smooth, mellow flavour with a delightful long-lasting finish.
Comments	Good after-dinner dram, and a malt which is rapidly gaining in popularity.

PERSONAL NOTES

Brand	CLYNELISH *(Kline-leesh)*
Distillery	Clynelish BRORA, Sutherland
Licensees	Ainslie & Heilbron (Distillers Ltd)
Reception centre	No. Visiting by appointment. Tel: 0408-21444.
Producing region	Highland, Northern
Age when bottled	12 years
Strength	40%

TASTING NOTES

Nose	Quite peaty for a Northern malt.
Taste	Rich, pleasant with a slightly dry finish — lots of character.
Comments	Good after-dinner malt. Popular amongst the connoisseurs.

PERSONAL NOTES

Malt	COLEBURN
Distillery	Coleburn Longmorn, ELGIN, Morayshire
Licensees	J&G Stewart Ltd
Reception centre	No
Producing region	Highland, Speyside

TASTING NOTES *(14 year old, 46%)*

Nose	Light and flowery.
Taste	Light and pleasant with a well rounded refreshing aftertaste.
Comments	Only available from the independent bottlers (see page 116).

PERSONAL NOTES

Talisker Distillery (see page 102)

Malt	CONVALMORE
Distillery	Convalmore DUFFTOWN, Banffshire
Licensees	WP Lowrie & Co Ltd
Reception centre	No
Producing region	Highland, Speyside

TASTING NOTES (19 year old, 46%)

Nose	Delicate and aromatic.
Taste	More pronounced than the aroma suggests. Pleasant roundness and full on the palate.
Comments	An after-dinner malt from the independent bottlers (see page 116).

PERSONAL NOTES

Malt	# CRAGGANMORE
Distillery	Cragganmore BALLINDALLOCH, Banffshire
Licensees	D&J McCallum Ltd
Reception centre	Yes. Visiting by appointment. Tel: 08072-202.
Producing region	Highland, Speyside

TASTING NOTES (1970 distillation)

Nose	Dry aroma, quite austere.
Taste	Good firm body with a malty-smokey finish.
Comments	Available at the distillery or from the independent bottlers (see page 116). After-dinner.

PERSONAL NOTES

Malt	CRAIGELLACHIE
Distillery	Craigellachie CRAIGELLACHIE, Banffshire
Licensees	White Horse Distillers Ltd
Reception Centre	No
Producing region	Highland, Speyside

TASTING NOTES (22 year old, 46%)

Nose	Pungent, smokey.
Taste	Light-bodied, smokey flavour. More delicate on the palate than the nose suggests. Good character.
Comments	After-dinner, but only available from the independent bottlers (see page 116).

PERSONAL NOTES

Bruichladdich Distillery (see page 23)

Malt	DAILUAINE
Distillery	Dailuaine CARRON, Morayshire
Licensees	Scottish Malt Distillers Ltd
Reception centre	No, but visitors are welcome.
Producing region	Highland, Speyside

TASTING NOTES (18 year old, 46%)

Nose	Very pungent and smokey.
Taste	Robust, full of flavour with a lingering finish. Excellent balance of flavour and taste.
Comments	A good after-dinner dram from the independent bottlers (see page 116).

PERSONAL NOTES

Lagavulin Distillery (see page 90)

Malt	DALLAS DHU *(Dallas-Doo)*
Distillery	Dallas Dhu FORRES, Morayshire
Licensees	Benmore Distilleries Ltd
Reception centre	No
Producing region	Highland, Speyside

TASTING NOTES *(21 year old, 46%)*

Nose	Delicate touch of peat.
Taste	Full-bodied, lingering flavour and smooth aftertaste.
Comments	Only available from the independent bottlers (see page 116). An after-dinner dram.

PERSONAL NOTES

40% Vol   **75 cl**

Brand	**DALWHINNIE**
Distillery	Dalwhinnie DALWHINNIE, Inverness-shire
Licensees	James Buchanan & Co Ltd
Reception Centre	Provisional. Tel: 05282-264.
Producing region	Highland, Northern
Age when bottled	15 years
Strength	*40%*

TASTING NOTES (18 year old, 46%)

Nose	A light aromatic bouquet.
Taste	Light with a thin heather-honey finish. Easy to drink.
Comments	Pre-dinner, available at the distillery and recently introduced to the U.K.

PERSONAL NOTES

Brand	DUFFTOWN
Distillery	Dufftown DUFFTOWN, Banffshire
Licensees	Arthur Bell & Sons PLC
Reception centre	No
Producing region	Highland, Speyside
Age when bottled	8 years
Strength	40%

TASTING NOTES

Nose	Light, flowery, pleasant aroma.
Taste	Good, round, smooth taste which tends to linger on the palate.
Comments	Pre-dinner.

PERSONAL NOTES

Malt	GLEN ALBYN
Distillery	Glen Albyn INVERNESS, Inverness-shire
Licensees	Scottish Malt Distillers Ltd
Reception centre	No
Producing region	Highland, Northern

TASTING NOTES (20 year old, 46%)

Nose	Light and smokey. Pleasant.
Taste	Well rounded, smokey with a full finish.
Comments	Only available from the independent bottlers (see page 116).

PERSONAL NOTES

Brand	**GLENDULLAN**
Distillery	Glendullan DUFFTOWN, Banffshire
Licensees	Macdonald Greenlees Ltd
Reception centre	No
Producing region	Highland, Speyside
Age when bottled	12 years
Strength	43%

TASTING NOTES

Nose	Attractive, fruity bouquet.
Taste	Firm, mellow with a delightful finish and a smooth lingering aftertaste.
Comments	Not very well known, but a good after-dinner malt.

PERSONAL NOTES

Brand	GLEN ELGIN
Distillery	Glen Elgin Longmorn, ELGIN, Morayshire
Licensees	White Horse Distillers Ltd
Reception centre	No
Producing region	Highland, Speyside
Age when bottled	12 years
Strength	43%

TASTING NOTES

Nose	Agreeable aroma of heather and honey.
Taste	Medium-weight touch of sweetness which finishes smoothly.
Comments	The best of both worlds, an excellent all round malt, suitable for drinking at any time.

PERSONAL NOTES

Brand	**GLEN ESK**
Distillery	Glen Esk Hillside, MONTROSE, Angus
Licensees	Wm Sanderson & Son Ltd
Reception centre	No
Producing region	Highland, Eastern
Age when bottled	12 years
Strength	40%

TASTING NOTES

Nose	A light, delicate hint of sweetness.
Taste	Quite full and sweet with a lingering finish, well balanced.
Comments	After-dinner. The distillery was once known as North Esk and also as Hillside.

PERSONAL NOTES

Malt	**GLENKINCHIE**
Distillery	Glenkinchie PENCAITLAND, East Lothian
Licensees	John Haig & Co Ltd
Reception centre	Yes, and a museum. Tel: 0875-340333.
Producing region	Lowland

TASTING NOTES (18 year old, 46%)

Nose	Clean aroma with a slight aromatic nose.
Taste	Light, spicy flavour, tending to finish quickly, yet always smoothly.
Comments	Available only from the independent bottlers (see page 117).

PERSONAL NOTES

Malt	GLENLOCHY
Distillery	Glenlochy FORT WILLIAM, Inverness-shire
Licensees	Scottish Malt Distillers Ltd
Reception centre	No
Producing region	Highland, Western

TASTING NOTES *(26 year old, 46%)*

Nose	Light and aromatic.
Taste	Light, spicy flavour which tends to finish quickly.
Comments	Pre-dinner drinking, but only from the independent bottlers (see page 117).

PERSONAL NOTES

Ardbeg Distillery (see page 104)

Malt	**GLENLOSSIE**
Distillery	Glenlossie-Glenlivet ELGIN, Morayshire
Licensees	John Haig & Co Ltd
Reception centre	No
Producing region	Highland, Speyside

TASTING NOTES *(18 year old, 46%)*

Nose	Soft touch of sweetness with a suggestion of sandalwood.
Taste	Soft and mellow with a long-lasting aromatic aftertaste.
Comments	Again, only available from the independent bottlers (see page 117).

PERSONAL NOTES

Malt	GLEN MHOR *(Glen Vawr)*
Distillery	Glen Mhor INVERNESS, Inverness-shire
Licensees	Scottish Malt Distillers Ltd
Reception Centre	No
Producing region	Highland, Northern

TASTING NOTES (8 year old, 40%)

Nose	Light, sweet fragrance.
Taste	Light-bodied with a slightly dry finish.
Comments	Good, all-round drinking from the independent bottlers (see page 117).

PERSONAL NOTES

Port Ellen Distillery and Maltings (see page 96)

Brand	**GLENORDIE** *(formerly ORD)*
Distillery	Ord
	MUIR of ORD, Ross-shire
Licensees	John Dewar & Son Ltd
Reception centre	Yes. Tel: 0463-870421.
Producing region	Highland, Northern
Age when bottled	12 years
Strength	40%

TASTING NOTES

Nose	A beautifully deep nose, with a tinge of dryness.
Taste	Good depth with a long-lasting, delicious aftertaste. Very smooth.
Comments	After-dinner.

PERSONAL NOTES

Malt	**GLENTAUCHERS**
Distillery	Glentauchers MULBEN, Banffshire
Licensees	James Buchanan & Co Ltd
Reception centre	No
Producing region	Highland, Speyside

TASTING NOTES (20 year old, 46%)

Nose	Light, sweet aroma.
Taste	Lightly flavoured with a light, dry finish.
Comments	A pre-dinner dram from the independent bottlers (see page 117).

PERSONAL NOTES

Brand	**GLENURY-ROYAL**
Distillery	Glenury-Royal STONEHAVEN, Kincardineshire
Licensees	John Gillon & Co Ltd
Reception centre	No
Producing region	Highland, Eastern
Age when bottled	12 years
Strength	40%

TASTING NOTES

Nose	A light hint of smoke with a dry aroma.
Taste	Light body with a dry, smokey finish.
Comments	A good introductory malt, suitable for pre-dinner drinking.

PERSONAL NOTES

Malt	IMPERIAL
Distillery	Imperial CARRON, Morayshire
Licensees	Scottish Malt Distillers Ltd
Reception centre	No
Producing region	Highland, Speyside

TASTING NOTES *(1969 distillation)*

Nose	Delightful — rich and smokey.
Taste	Rich and mellow with an absolutely delicious finish. A malt of real character.
Comments	After-dinner, again only from the independent bottlers (see page 117).

PERSONAL NOTES

Brand	**INCHGOWER**
Distillery	Inchgower BUCKIE, Banffshire
Licensees	Arthur Bell & Sons PLC
Reception centre	Planned for the near future.
Producing region	Highland, Speyside
Age when bottled	12 years
Strength	40%

TASTING NOTES

Nose	Very distinctive with a pleasant hint of sweetness.
Taste	Good, distinctive flavour finishing with a light sweetness.
Comments	A well balanced malt. After-dinner.

PERSONAL NOTES

Malt	KNOCKDHU *(Knock-doo)*
Distillery	Knockdhu KNOCK, Banffshire
Licensees	James Munro & Son Ltd
Reception Centre	No
Producing region	Highland, Speyside

TASTING NOTES *(1974 distillation)*

Nose	A quite distinctive, dry aroma.
Taste	Medium-bodied, round and gentle on the palate with a pleasant lingering taste.
Comments	After-dinner. Only available from the independent bottlers (see page 117).

PERSONAL NOTES

BY APPOINTMENT TO HER MAJESTY THE QUEEN
SCOTCH WHISKY DISTILLERS

WHITE HORSE DISTILLERS LTD. GLASGOW

LAGAVULIN

·estab·   ·1742·

ISLAY MALT
—scotch whisky—
The Lagavulin distillery was founded
in 1742. In gaelic it means 'hollow of the mill'.
Mountain air, moorland peat and
pure spring water give this malt its highly
distinctive character.

SPECIALLY SELECTED

DISTILLED AND BOTTLED IN SCOTLAND

43% vol   e 75 cl

Brand	LAGAVULIN *(Lagga-voolin)*
Distillery	Lagavulin PORT ELLEN, Islay, Argyll
Licensees	White Horse Distillers Ltd
Reception centre	Yes. Visiting by appointment. Tel: 0496-2400.
Producing region	Islay
Age when bottled	12 years
Strength	43%

THE
MALT
CELLAR
A collection of Scotland's
finest Malt Whiskies

TASTING NOTES

Nose	A typical Islay — heavy, powerful aroma. Unmistakable.
Taste	Robust, heavy, smokey and pungent. To be sipped and savoured to get the best of its dominating character.
Comments	The taste can take some acquiring, but a discriminating drinker's delight. Available everywhere.

PERSONAL NOTES

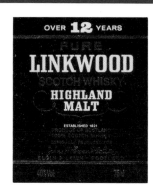

Brand	LINKWOOD
Distillery	Linkwood ELGIN, Morayshire
Licensees	John McEwan & Co Ltd
Reception centre	No. Visiting by appointment. Tel: 0343-7004.
Producing region	Highland, Speyside
Age when bottled	12 years
Strength	40%

TASTING NOTES

Nose	Slightly smokey with a trace of sweetness.
Taste	Full-bodied hint of sweetness.
Comments	One of the best malts available.

PERSONAL NOTES

Malt	MILLBURN
Distillery	Millburn INVERNESS, Inverness-shire
Licensees	Macleay Duff (Distillers) Ltd
Reception centre	No
Producing region	Highland, Northern

TASTING NOTES (13 year old, 46%)

Nose	A rich aroma with a faint sweetness.
Taste	Full-bodied, a touch of fruit and a good long finish.
Comments	Only from the independent bottlers (see page 117).

PERSONAL NOTES

Malt	MORTLACH
Distillery	Mortlach DUFFTOWN, Banffshire
Licensees	George Cowie & Sons Ltd
Reception centre	No
Producing region	Highland, Speyside

TASTING NOTES *(12 year old, 40%)*

Nose	A pleasant, well-rounded aroma.
Taste	Medium-bodied with a well balanced delightful finish.
Comments	A first class after-dinner malt from the independent bottlers (see page 117).

PERSONAL NOTES

Jura Distillery (see page 26)

Malt	NORTH PORT
Distillery	North Port BRECHIN, Angus
Licensees	Mitchell Bros Ltd
Reception centre	No
Producing region	Highland, Eastern

TASTING NOTES (17 year old, 46%)

Nose	A rather sharp, pronounced aroma, pricklish.
Taste	Starts sweet, but quickly fades to spirit — quite a sharp tang.
Comments	Pre-dinner, and preferably with water. Available only from the independent bottlers (see page 117).

PERSONAL NOTES

Tobermory Distillery (see page 57)

Brand	OBAN
Distillery	Oban OBAN, Argyll
Licensees	John Hopkins & Co Ltd
Reception centre	No. Limited capability. Visiting only by prior appointment. Tel: 0631-62110.
Producing region	Highland, Western
Age when bottled	12 years
Strength	40%

TASTING NOTES

Nose	Fresh, delicate hint of peat.
Taste	Medium body with a smooth finish and good long-lasting taste.
Comments	Good, all-round malt.

PERSONAL NOTES

Malt	**PORT ELLEN**
Distillery	Port Ellen PORT ELLEN, Islay, Argyll
Licensees	Low, Robertson & Co Ltd
Reception centre	No
Producing region	Islay

TASTING NOTES (1969 distillation)

Nose	A hint of peat with a delicate bouquet.
Taste	Light for an Islay, lacking that characteristic peaty flavour. A dry finish.
Comments	A popular pre-dinner dram from the independent bottlers (see page 117). Direct exports to the Americas were first pioneered at Port Ellen in the 1840s.

PERSONAL NOTES

Brand	ROSEBANK
Distillery	Rosebank Camelon, FALKIRK, Stirlingshire
Licensees	The Distiller's Agency Ltd
Reception centre	No. Visiting by appointment Tel: 0324-23325.
Producing region	Lowland
Age when bottled	8 years
Strength	40%

TASTING NOTES

Nose	Light, yet delicate.
Taste	Well balanced, good flavour with entirely acceptable astringency.
Comments	A triple-distilled malt suitable for pre-dinner drinking.

PERSONAL NOTES

Malt	ROYAL BRACKLA
Distillery	Royal Brackla NAIRN, Morayshire
Licensees	John Bisset & Co Ltd
Reception centre	No
Producing region	Highland, Northern

TASTING NOTES (18 year old, 46%)

Nose	A complex balance of peat and smoke with a touch of sweetness.
Taste	Big, and the peaty-smokey nose comes through on the palate with a hint of fruit and a dry finish.
Comments	An after-dinner dram only from the independent bottlers (see page 117).

PERSONAL NOTES

Brand	# ROYAL LOCHNAGAR
Distillery	Lochnagar Crathie, BALLATER, Aberdeenshire
Licensees	John Begg Ltd
Reception centre	Provisional. Visiting by appointment. Tel: 03384-273.
Producing region	Highland, Eastern
Age when bottled	12 years
Strength	40%

TASTING NOTES

Nose	Pleasant, full nose.
Taste	Good, full body with a clean wholesome taste. Delicate trace of sweetness.
Comments	After-dinner.

PERSONAL NOTES

Malt	SPEYBURN
Distillery	Speyburn ROTHES, Morayshire
Licensees	John Robertson & Son Ltd
Reception centre	No
Producing region	Highland, Speyside

TASTING NOTES (16 year old, 46%)

Nose	A heather-honey bouquet.
Taste	Big, full-bodied malty taste with a sweet finish.
Comments	After-dinner. From the independent bottlers only (see page 117).

PERSONAL NOTES

Malt	ST MAGDALENE
Distillery	St Magdalene LINLITHGOW, West Lothian
Licensees	Wm Greer & Co Ltd
Reception centre	No
Producing region	Lowland

TASTING NOTES *(20 year old, 46%)*

Nose	A round aroma with a touch of smoke.
Taste	Full-bodied, smooth with a rich finish and much character.
Comments	After-dinner malt. Again only from the independent bottlers (see page 117).

PERSONAL NOTES

Bunnahabhain Distillery (see page 16)

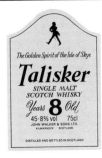

Brand	TALISKER
Distillery	Talisker CARBOST, Isle of Skye
Licensees	John Walker & Sons Ltd
Reception centre	Yes. Tel: 047842-203.
Producing region	Island, Skye
Age when bottled	8 years
Strength	45.8%

TASTING NOTES

Nose	Peaty, well balanced sweet aroma.
Taste	Round, full flavour which explodes on the palate, lingering on and on. Totally unique.
Comments	Superb after-dinner malt, one of the best.

PERSONAL NOTES

Malt	**TEANINICH**
Distillery	Teaninich ALNESS, Ross-shire
Licensees	RH Thompson & Co (Distillers) Ltd
Reception centre	No
Producing region	Highland, Northern

TASTING NOTES *(26 year old, 46%)*

Nose	Subtle, fruity with a gentle bouquet.
Taste	Soft, full of flavour and a delight to drink. Really warms the palate.
Comments	A good pre-dinner malt from the independent bottlers (see page 117).

PERSONAL NOTES

Hiram Walker & Sons (Scotland) PLC

3 High St, DUMBARTON G82 1ND

Tel: 0389-65111

Brand	ARDBEG
Distillery	Ardbeg PORT ELLEN, Islay, Argyll
Licensees	Ardbeg Distillery Ltd
Reception centre	No
Producing region	Islay
Age when bottled	10 years
Strength	40%

TASTING NOTES

Nose	Lovely peaty aroma with a hint of sweetness.
Taste	Full-bodied and luscious with an excellent aftertaste.
Comments	Good after-dinner malt. Perhaps the ultimate test for beginners?

PERSONAL NOTES

Brand	**BALBLAIR**
Distillery	Balblair Edderton, TAIN, Ross-shire
Licensees	George Ballantine & Son Ltd
Reception centre	No
Producing region	Highland, Northern
Age when bottled	5 years
Strength	40%

TASTING NOTES

Nose	Delightful, light fragrance of peat.
Taste	Good lingering flavour, long-lasting with a slender hint of sweetness.
Comments	A fine dram anytime. Now bottled by Ballantines and available on the UK market.

PERSONAL NOTES

GLENBURGIE

PRODUCT OF SCOTLAND

GLENBURGIE-GLENLIVET

100%
Highland Malt
Scotch Whisky

5 YEARS OLD

DISTILLED & BOTTLED IN SCOTLAND

The Glenburgie-Glenlivet Distillery Co.
Forres, Scotland

ESTABLISHED 1810

Brand	GLENBURGIE
Distillery	Glenburgie-Glenlivet FORRES, Morayshire
Licensees	James and George Stodart Ltd
Reception centre	No
Producing region	Highland, Speyside
Age when bottled	5 years, but only occasionally available.
Strength	40%

TASTING NOTES *(18 year old, 46%)*

Nose	A fragrant, herbal aroma.
Taste	A light, delicate aromatic flavour with a pleasant finish.
Comments	Usually bottled for export only. A good pre-dinner malt.

PERSONAL NOTES

Malt	GLENCADAM
Distillery	Glencadam BRECHIN, Angus
Licensees	George Ballantine & Sons Ltd
Reception centre	No
Producing region	Highland, Eastern

TASTING NOTES *(14 year old, 46%)*

Nose	Light hint of sweetness.
Taste	Full, with quite a fruity flavour and a good finish.
Comments	An after-dinner malt which is only available from the independent bottlers (see page 116).

PERSONAL NOTES

Malt	**INVERLEVEN**
Distillery	Inverleven DUMBARTON, Strathclyde
Licensees	Hiram Walker & Sons (Scotland) PLC
Reception centre	No
Producing region	Lowland

TASTING NOTES *(17 year old, 46%)*

Nose	Delicate hint of smoke.
Taste	Quite full-bodied. Smooth, with a round palate.
Comments	Rarely available unless obtained from the independent bottlers (see page 117).

PERSONAL NOTES

Brand	MILTON DUFF
Distillery	Miltonduff-Glenlivet ELGIN, Morayshire
Licensees	George Ballantine & Sons Ltd
Reception centre	Yes
Producing region	Highland
Age when bottled	12 years
Strength	43%

TASTING NOTES

Nose	Agreeable, fragrant bouquet.
Taste	Medium-bodied with a pleasant, well matured, subtle finish.
Comments	After-dinner. Another malt called **Mosstowie** used to be produced from Lomond type stills at Milton Duff and is available from the independent bottlers (see page 117).

PERSONAL NOTES

Malt	PULTENEY *(Pult-nay)*
Distillery	Pulteney WICK, Caithness
Licensees	James & George Stodart Ltd
Reception centre	No
Producing region	Highland, Northern

TASTING NOTES *(8 year old, 40%)*

Nose	Fine, delicate, light aroma with an ozone-like bouquet.
Taste	Light, crisp, refreshing finish.
Comments	An excellent aperitif whisky but only available from the independent bottlers as **Old Pulteney** (see page 117). The most northerly mainland distillery.

PERSONAL NOTES

Malt	SCAPA
Distillery	Scapa KIRKWALL, Orkney
Licensees	Taylor & Ferguson Ltd
Reception centre	No
Producing region	Island, Orkney

TASTING NOTES *(8 year old, 40%)*

Nose	Delightful aromatic bouquet of peat and heather.
Taste	Medium-bodied with a malty, silk-like finish.
Comments	After-dinner, but only from the independent bottlers (see page 117). The Navy rescued Scapa from destruction by fire during the First World War!

PERSONAL NOTES

Whyte & Mackay Distillers Ltd

Dalmore House, 296/298 St. Vincent Street

GLASGOW G2 5RG

Tel: 041-248-5771

Brand	DALMORE
Distillery	Dalmore ALNESS, Ross-shire
Licensees	Whyte & Mackay Distillers Ltd
Reception centre	No
Producing region	Highland, Northern
Age when bottled	12 years
Strength	40%

TASTING NOTES

Nose	Rich, fresh, with a suggestion of sweetness.
Taste	Full flavour which finishes a touch dry.
Comments	Another really good malt. After-dinner.

PERSONAL NOTES

Brand	OLD FETTERCAIRN
Distillery	Fettercairn FETTERCAIRN, Kincardineshire
Licensees	Whyte & Mackay Distillers Ltd
Reception centre	No
Producing region	Highland, Eastern
Age when bottled	None given
Strength	40%

TASTING NOTES

Nose	Light, fresh aroma.
Taste	Fresh, stimulating finish with a touch of dryness.
Comments	A good all-round drink.

PERSONAL NOTES

Brand	**TOMINTOUL-GLENLIVET** *(Tommin-towl)*
Distillery	Tomintoul-Glenlivet BALLINDALLOCH, Banffshire
Licensees	Whyte & Mackay Distillers Ltd
Reception centre	No
Producing region	Highland, Speyside
Age when bottled	None given
Strength	40%, 43% for export.

TASTING NOTES

Nose	Light and delicate.
Taste	Light body with good character.
Comments	A good introduction to malt. Bottled in an interesting manner for export.

PERSONAL NOTES

VATTED MALTS

A vatted malt is frequently a marriage of four or five quality single malts, each one enhancing the quality of the others so that the sum is greater than the parts.

The object is to produce a branded malt whisky which is consistent in flavour and quality at all times, whereas a single malt may, due to varying climatic conditions at the time of distillation, show some degree of change in nose and flavour. There are numerous vatted malts available and I have chosen Strathconon as one of the more popular brands.

James Buchanan & Co Ltd

Brand	STRATHCONON

TASTING NOTES *(12 year old, 40%)*

Nose	Pleasant malt nose.
Taste	Good weight with a well balanced mellow flavour and a hint of dryness at the end.
Comments	After-dinner.

PERSONAL NOTES

INDEPENDENT BOTTLERS

The following malts are not marketed as brands
by their respective distillers and are available
from the two main Scottish independent bottlers:

Gordon & MacPhail Ltd

58 - 60 South Street
ELGIN
Morayshire IV30 1JY
Tel: 0343-45111
Gordon and MacPhail usually give the year of
distillation instead of the age when bottled.
Strength is normally 40% alcohol by volume.

William Cadenhead Ltd

32 Union St
CAMPBELTOWN, Argyll PA28 6HY
Tel: 0586-52009
William Cadenhead bottle malts at 46% alcohol
by volume and at a number of ages.

	G & M	Wm Cad
Aberfeldy	1969	
Ardmore		18 years old
Balmenach	1970	24 years old
Ben Nevis		19 years old
Benriach	1969	13, 21 years old
Benrinnes	1968	23 years old
Benromach	1968	14, 18 years old
Caol Ila	1969	
Caperdonich	1979	18 years old
Coleburn	1972	14, 17 years old
Convalmore	1969	23 years old
Cragganmore	1970/71/72	
Craigellachie	1971	22 years old
Dailuaine	1971	22 years old
Dallas Dhu	1969	21 years old
Glen Albyn	1963	20 years old
Glencadam	1974	16, 25 years old
Glenglassaugh	1967	
Glen Keith	1963/65	17 years old

	G & M	Wm Cad
Glenkinchie	1964	
Glenlochy	1974	15, 26 years old
Glenlossie	1968/69	18 years old
Glen Mhor	8,15 years old	20 years old
Glenrothes	1955/56	16 years old
Glentauchers		20 years old
Glenugie	1966	14, 20 years old
Imperial	1970	
Inverleven		17 years old
Kinclaith	1966/67	20 years old
Knockdhu	1974	
Ladyburn		14 years old
Ledaig	1972	
Lochside	1965/66	
Macduff	1963	13, 21 years old
Millburn	1966	13 years old
Mortlach	12, 21, 25 years old	25 years old
Mosstowie	1970	
North Port	1970	17 years old
Old Pulteney	8, 15 years old; 1961	
Port Ellen	1970	
Royal Brackla	1969	18 years old
Scapa	8 years old 1960	20 years old
Speyburn	1968	16 years old
St Magdalene	1964	20, 23 years old
Teaninich	1969/71	27 years old

PERSONAL NOTES
AUCHENTOSHAN (page 42)

BRUICHLADDICH (page 23)

GLEN DEVERON (page 31)

GLENFARCLAS (page 13)

GLENMORANGIE (page 38)

PERSONAL NOTES
GLENTURRET (page 12)

INCHMURRIN (page 11)

LONGROW (page 40)

MACALLAN (page 37)

SPRINGBANK (page 41)

INDEX